MCC

MCC

MUSICAL INSTRUMENTS

Meryl Doney

FRANKLIN WATTS

A Division of Grolier Publishing

NEW YORK • LONDON • HONG KONG • SYDNEY
DANBURY, CONNECTICUT

About this book

When you begin to study musical instruments from around the world you will be amazed at the number of ways that people have discovered for making music. They range from beating out a rhythm on a piece of wood to the astonishing *gamelan* orchestra of Java in Indonesia. In every country, musicians have made use of local materials and methods to make their own music.

At the same time, it is striking to see how the same types of instrument occur on all the continents of the world. Making music is a very important activity. It brings people together in a unique way, and it is easy to see how musicians have shared their secrets and spread ideas from country to country.

In this book you will find examples of many different kinds of instrument, as well as maps to show where each one comes from. These instruments represent only a fraction of the rich variety in the world. If you would like to know more, there is a list of helpful books at the back of this book.

We will show you many different methods for making the instruments, beginning with the simplest and going on to the more complex. Most of the steps are very easy to follow, but where you see this sign ask for help from an adult.

Of course, musical instruments are not just decorative. They have to work. You will need patience and perseverance both to make them and to learn how to play them well. As you become more confident, add colors, decorations, and modifications of your own. In this way musicians have developed new versions of old favorites.

Music to entertain

Music making is a wonderful way of bringing people together, and you can gain much enjoyment from entertaining others. When you have made some instruments and have become reasonably good at playing them, you might like to gather a group of family or friends together to form an orchestra or band (see page 29).

First published in the United States
in 1995 by Franklin Watts
Text © 1995 by Meryl Doney

Franklin Watts
90 Sherman Turnpike
Danbury, CT 06813

10 9 8 7 6 5 4 3 2 1

Series editor: Annabel Martin
Editor: Jane Walker
Design: Visual Image
Cover design: Chloë Cheesman / Mike Davis
Artwork: Ruth Levy
Photography: Peter Millard

Library of Congress Cataloging-in-Publication Data

Doney, Meryl, 1942-
    Musical Instruments / Meryl Doney.
        p.   cm. − (World crafts)
    includes bibliographical references (p.   ) and index.
    Summary: Provides step-by-step instructions for making a variety of musical instruments from around the world, including Mexican rhythm sticks, Ethiopian bells and a paper prayer drum from India.
        ISBN 0-531-14398-8   (lib. bdg.)
        ISBN 0-531-15871-3   (pbk)
    1. Musical Instruments − Construction − Juvenile literature.
    [1. Musical Instruments − Construction.] I. Title. II. Series.
    MI460.D58   1995   95-18099
    784.192'3−dc20   CIP
                                             AC MN

Printed in Great Britain

Contents

A musical history

Making music is as old as the human race itself. No one can tell exactly when musical instruments were first used, except that people probably used themselves as instruments right from the beginning! They would clap their hands, stamp their feet, and of course, use their voices.

People in ancient times used natural objects to make different sounds — wood on wood, wood on stone, bone on stone. Simple rhythm instruments are known to have existed in Europe as far back as 25,000 years ago — that's around 23,000 B.C!

People have also been using wind instruments for a very long time. Early flutes and horns were generally used in religious ceremonies or as a means for people to signal to one another. As civilizations became more developed in the Middle East and Europe, more sophisticated instruments were made. They began to be used for entertainment as well.

Music has been made in every culture. It is used for religious worship, important family and state occasions, parties, and entertainment. Although musical styles differ from period to period and from one culture to another, the kind of instruments that people make are remarkably similar worldwide. Drums, flutes, horns, rattles, and stringed instruments appear just about everywhere.

Instruments can be made simply from local materials, or by using the most complicated computer technology. All it takes to play some instruments well is a good sense of timing and rhythm, while others need years of practice. In either case, the joy that people get from playing and listening to music is equally worthwhile.

Your own music-making kit

Many of the instruments in this book are made from natural materials. Others use manufactured items like cardboard tubes, tin cans, and bottle tops. Put together your own music-making kit by collecting materials you may need. Keep small items in plastic tubs and the rest in a big cardboard box, together with a set of tools.

Here are some of the most useful items for your music-making kit:

hammer • small saw • vise • nail with a large head • hand drill • pliers • wood file or rasp • scissors • mat knife • metal ruler • brushes • gesso • poster paints • varnish • PVA (white) glue • tube of strong glue • plastic modeling material • modeling clay • wood •

dowel • wire • leather • bamboo • string • masking tape • paper • pen • pencil • felt-tip pens • needle and thread • metal skewer • nails • wooden block to hammer on • sandpaper • newspaper to work on • protective gloves • apron • paper towels for cleaning up

Ideas for decoration

When you have made a musical instrument you can invent your own style of decoration. Try using different colors, patterns, and shapes. If the instruments come from a culture different from your own and you need some inspiration, visit your local or school library. Look for a book about the particular country or people that interest you.

See if you can find the different ways in which they decorate the things they make.

Trace patterns and shapes, or adapt them freely for your own use. We have used this method for the prayer drum on page 25. The design was taken from one sewn in beads on the back of a North American Indian baby carrier, called a cradleboard.

Sticks and stones

Rhythm is essential to making music, and clapping is one of the simplest means of keeping a beat. Some of the first musical instruments that people invented were designed to do their clapping for them! In ancient Egypt ivory clappers were made with just that purpose in mind.

We still use this method to beat out a rhythm. The modern wooden clappers shown below left are made by the Aboriginal people of Australia. They are carved from hardwood and a hot metal skewer is used to burn in the decorations.

Shakers or rattles can also be made from sea or animal shells, hide and leather, horn, wood, and metal. Leg rattles like the one on the right are called *amahlwayi*. They are made from insect cocoons by the Ndebele tribe of Zimbabwe. The Mexican scraper (above), which is called a *guiro*, is sounded by running a stick along the ridges that are cut into the wood.

Instruments that make use of the sounds made by natural objects such as stone, wood, or metal, are called ideophones. They can be played by stamping with the feet, shaking, rattling, hitting with another object, banging or scraping together, or plucking.

Make your own rhythm sticks

You will need: 16 in (40 cm) dowel • small saw • vise • sandpaper • wood file or rasp • protective gloves • metal meat skewer • pliers • poster paints • varnish

Can you think of other ideas for sound makers? Gently tap as many things as you can find with a dowel beater. Be careful not to try anything fragile. Most materials have a natural note when sounded. Here are some suggestions: juice bottles (the note can be altered by pouring in some water), saucepan lids, radiators, wastebaskets, tiles, a nail hung on a string, wooden floorboards, and tin trays.

1 Grip dowel in vise and saw off two 8-in (20-cm) lengths.

2 Smooth ends with sandpaper or shape to a point with file or rasp.

3 To decorate sticks Aboriginal style, put on protective gloves. Grip skewer in pliers and hold in a gas flame until very hot. Lay hot skewer across wood in vise so that it burns a brown mark. The end of the skewer makes a round dot.

Repeat, making more marks, to form a pattern. When finished, run cold water over skewer to cool it.

4 Alternatively, you can decorate your sticks by painting and varnishing them.

You could make a *guiro* scraper by wrapping and tying string around a large plastic bottle. Then scrape it with a stick.

Shake and rattle

When a gourd or a seed pod dries in the sun, the flesh shrivels up leaving the hard seeds to rattle around inside. These natural rattles have long been used in music and magical rituals. The black gourd rattle from Southern Africa (right) is a good example.

A gourd is also the basis for the *kass-kassa* (sometimes called a *shekere* or *kabassa*). The one shown top right is made by Issifou Amadou in Togo. The calabash gourds are specially grown and trained to the correct shape. The covering is made from elephant grass seeds threaded on a string mesh. The shaker is held in the hand and the seeds are shaken against the surface or swirled around the gourd.

The handmade *tioco-tioco-ni* (pronounced "chiko-chiko-ni"), or basketwork shaker (above left), has a gourd or tin base. The seeds rattle against it. The shaker is obviously modeled on the shape of a gourd.

Weave a basket shaker

You will need: a compass • cork tile • hole punch • newspaper • mat knife • 15-in (38-cm) lengths of cane • string or raffia • ball • dried chick-peas or beans • masking tape

1 Use compass to draw two circles, radius 1½ and 2 in (3.6 and 4.6 cm), on tile. Set compass to ½ in (1 cm) and divide inner circle into 23 sections.

2 Lay tile on newspaper. Cut around outer circle with mat knife. Punch hole at each point on inner circle.

3 Soak cane in water until pliable. Push 2 in (5 cm) of each cane through each hole in the cork circle. Weave ends of cane together around base as shown.

4 On top side, tie end of string or raffia to base of a cane. Weave in and out, pushing string down as you go. Use different colors to build up stripes. Encourage your work to bend outward by putting a ball inside canes.

5 After 2½ in (6 cm) of weaving, remove ball and begin to draw weaving inward toward a point. Before closing rattle completely, drop in a handful of dried chick-peas or beans.

6 Divide ends of canes into two bunches and form into a circular handle. Secure with masking tape. Bind handle with string or raffia.

Handy hint: If craft cane is not available, buy a small basket at a craft store and unravel it.

Bells on their toes

Bells and jingles are examples of metal ideophones. Bells have a loose "clapper," which hits against the metal sides. They are often used by dancers because they emphasize the body's movements.

The *ghunghura* (right) are brass dancing bells from India. They can be worn around the ankle, wrist, or waist on a string or belt. Morris dancers in Britain use similar bells for their dances.

Metal jingles, which are similar to bells, have a long history in dance and as an aid to prayer and worship. The *sistrum*, which is a metal and wire shaker, can be traced back to ancient Egypt and Roman Pompeii. It is used today by the Coptic church of Ethiopia. The wooden *sistrum* below comes from Harare, Zimbabwe. It is made with recycled bottle-tops.

The tambourine above is also from Harare. Tambourines, or frame drums, originated in the Middle East.

Make a cake pan tambourine

You could make a *sistrum* from a branch with its bark removed. Use the same method as for the tambourine shown here. Put the branch in a vise and drill holes for the wire. Decorate using a hot skewer (see page 7), or paint and varnish.

You will need: small shallow tin cake pan • can opener • hammer • wooden block • file • felt-tip pen • awl • mat knife • bottle tops • pliers • plastic modeling material • coat hanger wire

1 Remove base of cake pan with can opener.

Hammer rough edges flat on wooden block. Smooth with file.

2 Mark a rectangle, 2 x 1 in (5 x 2.5 cm), on side of pan. Add a line down the center of the rectangle. Repeat at 2-in (5-cm) intervals until you have five rectangles.

3 Punch hole with awl halfway down each side of each rectangle as shown.

Cut along H-shape by pressing on pan with mat knife.

4 Hold each bottle top in pliers and beat flat with hammer on wooden block.

Place each bottle top on plastic modeling material and punch hole in center with awl.

5 Cut five 2-in (5-cm) pieces of wire. Inside pan, bend back two sides of rectangles to form tabs.

6 Thread wire through one hole, two bottle tops, and second hole. Flatten tabs with hammer to hold wire in place. Flatten sharp edges.

Hanging sounds

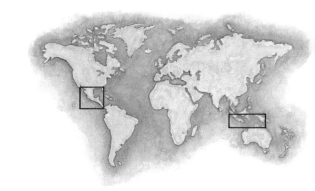

Wind chimes like these ones from Mexico are another form of ideophone. Natural objects like wood, stone, or fired clay have their own particular tone if suspended and allowed to vibrate freely. Try this for yourself. Tie a piece of cotton around a nail. Hold the nail up so that it does not touch anything else, then hit it with a dowel. It should make a ringing sound. Different-size nails make different notes.

This same principle is also used by the family of instruments that includes the xylophone (wooden bars), the lithophone (stone or slate), and the metalophone (metal). The bars are suspended above tubes or gourds that act as sound boxes.

Highly developed bar ideophones are found in the *gamelan* orchestras of Java and Bali in Indonesia. These orchestras provide music for shadow-puppet plays. Instruments in the *gamelan* include large gongs, which are suspended in decorated frames, and the *gender*, or wooden xylophone (right).

Make tile music

You will need: cereal box • scissors • five toilet paper tubes • glue • a length of balsa wood, $^3/_4$ x $^3/_4$ in (1.5 x 1.5 cm) • pencil • 12 1-in (2-cm) nails with flat heads • gesso • poster paints • varnish • five tile edging pieces • pliers • 10 small rubber bands

1 Cut cereal box to same height as cardboard tubes. Glue to inside of box.

2 Cut two strips of balsa wood the same length as cereal box. Hold strips alongside tubes. Mark dots at either end and between tubes. Knock nail into wood at each dot, leaving $^3/_4$ in (1.5 cm) of each nail sticking up.

3 Glue strips along top edges of box. Glue base of box to two short balsa strips as feet. Paint with gesso, decorate with poster paints, and varnish.

4 Keep one tile at full length. Shorten the next bar by gently breaking $^1/_2$ in (1 cm) off one end with a pair of pliers. Shorten the next by 1 in (2 cm) and so on until the fifth bar is 2 in (4 cm) shorter. (Be careful to wrap and throw away sharp pieces of tile.)

5 Stretch rubber bands between each nail along balsa on both sides. Suspend bars by twisting rubber bands and pushing bars between them along length of instrument as shown. Check note of each bar with a piano. Tune by removing a little more tile.

"Tongues" and thumbs

These instruments belong to the linguaphone family (from *lingua*, the Latin word for "tongue"). Sounds from the vibrating "tongue" are amplified by directing them into a confined space called a sound box, or resonator.

The Jew's (or jaw's) harp works by plucking a "tongue" which is held between two sides of a frame. The frame is placed between the player's teeth. The open mouth is the resonator and the pitch of the note is changed by moving the player's tongue or cheeks. This man from Pakistan is playing a jaw's harp.

The *mbira*, also called *sansa* or "thumb piano," originated in Africa. This one is from Kenya. It is held in the palms of the hands and the thumbs are used to pluck the "tongues." They are held tightly against a bridge on a piece of wood or a box. Often the wood is carved, painted, and decorated. Extra rattling sounds can be added by wrapping wire around the tongues or by nailing flattened bottle tops to the box.

Make a thumb piano

You need a length of bamboo cane to make a bamboo jaw's harp. Split the cane in half with a mat knife. Make two more cuts, leaving a tongue in between. Hold the harp in your teeth and pluck the tongue to make a note.

You will need: a piece of wooden board, 8 x $\frac{1}{2}$ x 5 in (20 x 1.5 x 12 cm) • pencil • ruler • V-shaped linoleum cutting tool • dark brown shoe polish • polishing cloth • pliers • coat hanger wire • hammer • 10 metal staples

1 Draw two lines 1 and 2 ins (3 and 4.5 cm) from end of board. Mark a pattern of lines on rest of surface. Carve pattern into wood with linoleum cutting tool. (Always work away from your hands.)

2 Polish wood with dark brown shoe polish. Rub off excess polish.

3 Cut seven pieces of coat hanger wire of different lengths, from 5 to 3$\frac{1}{2}$ ins (12 to 9 cm). Hold each one over a very hard surface with pliers. Beat ends flat with hammer. Cut two more pieces of wire 4 in (10 cm) long.

4 Lay one piece of 4-in (10-cm) wire along second line on wood and hammer in staple at each end. Lay all 7 tongues across this wire. Lay second piece of wire over tongues along first line. Staple at both ends and between each tongue. Check that tongues make a good, clear sound.

Flutes and whistles

Long ago, people discovered that they could make pleasant sounds by blowing air against a sharp edge. This caused the edge to vibrate. The musical instruments that use this principle are called aerophones. They range from simple penny whistles to the grandest church organ.

Bird-bone whistles and flutes have been found dating back to the Stone Age. The Andean Indians of South America believed that playing flutes made from the bones of your enemies gave you power over them. The ceramic flute (right) is a copy of one made by the Mayan peoples of Central America some 2,000 years ago. It is very similar to the recorder that is played in schools today. The little bird whistle above is from Costa Rica.

A sound can also be made by blowing over a hole in a round or shaped vessel. You can change the note by covering and uncovering other holes with your fingers. The round vessel flute (top left) works on this principle. It is made from a dried matamba fruit in Mozambique. The decorated ceramic flute (left), called an ocarina, comes from Peru.

Make a clay flute

You will need: modeling clay • knife • large needle • poster paints • varnish

1 Roll a piece of clay flat. Cut out two egg shapes, 3 in (7 cm) across and 3¹/₂ in (9 cm) long, and a rectangle 2 x 1 in (5 x 2 cm). Make a roll of clay 1 in (2 cm) long. Cut thin slice off side of roll.

2 Score edges of each clay piece with large needle and moisten with water. Form each egg into a bowl shape. Press the two shapes carefully together to form a hollow egg. Score edges together with the needle, leaving a gap at one end. Smooth join with a little water.

3 Form clay rectangle into short tube and attach it to egg by scoring. Push clay roll into tube, flat side up, leaving a gap to blow through. Smooth clay with dampened fingers.

4 Use needle to make four small holes in upper surface of egg shape. Make one larger hole on top, just behind blowing hole. Make two small holes in lower surface.

5 Check that the flute works before it dries hard. Cover four small holes with fingers and gently blow through end hole.

If flute does not whistle, adjust the edge of large hole. (The sound is made by blown air hitting the far edge of this hole.)

6 Leave to dry. Paint and varnish.

Pipes to blow

Many instruments have developed from the simple idea of blowing down a tube. The South American *zamponas* shown below are probably the best known. They are sometimes called panpipes because the Greek god Pan was always shown playing them. *Zamponas* are made up of small flutes that are crafted from bamboo grown in Bolivia. The flutes are joined together in a row. They have no fingerholes and are closed at one end.

Trumpets and horns are larger versions of the pipe. They are played by vibrating the lips together and using the pipe as the resonator. Horns, as their name suggests, were originally made from animal horns. Trumpets were made from any material that could be hollowed out, such as wood, bamboo, bark, or metal. The decorated gourd horn shown left is from Nigeria.

Another group of pipes uses a thin tongue, called a reed, to vibrate the air. The clarinet, oboe, bassoon, and bagpipes come into this category. The double clarinet below is from Syria.

Make some panpipes

This set of eight pipes will give you a scale of G major. You will need to tune each pipe as you make it, using a piano or recorder (see page 29). If the pipe sounds too low (flat), saw some more off its length. If it is too high (sharp), use it for the next pipe and make a new, longer one.

You will need: ½-in (1.5-cm) garden bamboo cane, at least 8 sections long • vise • saw • sandpaper • garden stick • ruler • pencil • heavy mat knife • thick twine

1 Grip garden cane in vise and cut into 8 sections just below each knot in bamboo. Remove pith from inside tubes with rolled-up sandpaper.

2 Use a garden stick as a gauge. Measure 4½ in (107 mm) from one end and make a mark. Push it down inside bamboo tube and mark length. Remove and hold alongside bamboo with length mark in place. Transfer 4½-in (107-mm) mark to bamboo. Use saw to cut bamboo at this mark.

3 Repeat this process, with the other 7 pipes, marking them at 3³/₄, 3¹/₄, 3, 2³/₄, 2¹/₂, 2¹/₄ and 2 in (94, 82, 77, 69, 61, 56 and 49 mm). Sand pipes until smooth and check notes (see above).

4 Cut another piece of bamboo, 5½ in (14 cm) long, with no knots. Split in half with mat knife.

5 Tie length of thick twine around longest pipe. Tie diagonally to half bamboo strip, wind around top and onto next pipe. Continue until all eight pipes are held firmly in place. Knot end of twine.

Strings and bows

The chordophones are another family of musical instruments. They include guitars, violins, and pianos. Chordophones rely on the vibration of strings to make sounds.

Very simple versions of the violin or fiddle are thought to have originated in Persia. Later, they spread to the Middle East, Asia, and North Africa. The round folk violin (left) comes from Mozambique. Its body is made from a calabash gourd and the skin still has animal hair attached to it.

The square-shaped folk violin (right) is called a *rebab*. It comes from Jordan. Violins of this type are known as spike fiddles because the neck runs through the body and out at the base as a spike. The *rebab* is held vertically, with the spike resting on the player's knee or on the floor. A bow made from a springy piece of wood is drawn across the string to play the instrument.

Make a one-string violin

This instrument is played by running a bow across the string to vibrate it. (See page 28 for instructions on making a bow.) You can change the note by pressing your finger on the neck end of the string.

You will need: coconut • skewer • plastic modeling material • protective gloves • small saw • penknife • sandpaper • vise • hand drill • ¹/₂-in (1-cm) dowel, 18¹/₂ in (47 cm) long • chamois leather • pencil • carpet tacks • stick • mat knife • guitar string or fuse wire • small bamboo ring • thin garden cane • string

1 Use the skewer to pierce two coconut "eyes" (flat areas near the point of the nut). Let milk drain out. Stand nut on plastic modeling material. Using protective gloves, hold nut firmly and ask an adult to saw it in half lengthwise.

2 Remove flesh from one half with a knife. Sand the outside of shell smooth.

3 Grip shell in vise and drill row of small holes ¹/₂ in (1 cm) from edge all round. Drill ¹/₂-in (1-cm) hole at both ends. Drill small hole ¹/₂ in (1 cm) from end of dowel and a larger one 3 in (7 cm) from end.

4 Draw around nut on chamois leather. Cut out shape ³/₄ in (2 cm) larger. Soak leather in water, squeeze out, and stretch over shell to form drum. Hammer tacks into small holes, stretching leather across nut. Trim off excess leather. Allow to dry.

5 Push dowel through two large holes so that end sticks out 1 in (3 cm). Whittle peg from stick and score groove across top. Push peg into larger hole. Thread guitar string through small hole, around dowel several times, and over groove in peg. Pull tight and tie around dowel spike. Add tension to wire by adding bridge made from grooved bamboo ring.

Guitars old and new

The modern-day guitar is closely related to the family of lutes and mandolins that have been popular all over the world for many hundreds of years. The Chinese *p'i p'a* (shown right) has been in existence for at least 2,000 years, and the Japanese *biwa* developed from it. This family of instruments has grown to include the European *bouzouki*, *tambura*, *balalaika*, and *bandoura*, and the Middle Eastern *ud*, *tambur*, and *krar*. In India the *sitar* and *surbahar* from the north, and the *tambura* and *mayuri* from the south, are all related.

The *ramkie* is a simple folk guitar from Southern Africa. The one shown above comes from Harare, Zimbabwe. It is made from an old oilcan.

Recycle an oilcan

1 Drain oil from can. Punch a number of large holes in front left side of can with awl.

You will need: large, square oilcan • hammer • awl • mat knife • detergent • two pieces of wood, $^3/_4$ x 2$^1/_2$ x 30 in and $^1/_2$ x $^3/_4$ x 2$^1/_2$ in (1.5 x 6 x 75 cm and 1 x 1.5 x 6 cm) • sandpaper • wood file or rasp • paint • wood drill • length of stick • nails • 4 guitar strings • thick rubber strip

2 Cut around three sides of a rectangle on top right side of can with heavy mat knife. Bend tab upright. Punch four holes through side and base of can on right side. Wash out can with detergent to remove rest of oil. Leave in warm place to dry inside.

3 Use sandpaper and file or rasp to smooth wooden fingerboard. Shape and round off top corners. Drill four holes for pegs. Paint and decorate if you like.

4 Cut four 2$^1/_2$-in (6-cm) lengths of stick. Whittle into tapering pegs with mat knife. Cut a deep groove in top of each peg. Cut four grooves into top of 2$^1/_2$-in (6-cm) wooden bridge.

5 Slot the fingerboard into oilcan and nail in place on base. Rest on edge of table and nail tab to fingerboard.

6 Tie guitar strings through holes in base and wind around pegs. Wedge pegs in holes and twist. Slip bridge under strings and rest it on can. Tune with piano or recorder.

7 To make a *capotasto* (a device for changing the key of the strings), cut slits in both ends and middle of rubber strip. Thread a 3$^1/_2$-in (9-cm) length of stick through two slits, and lay across strings. Wrap rubber behind board and slip third slit over end of stick.

Mini drums

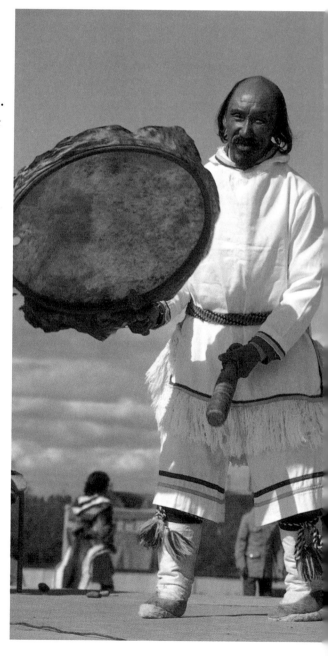

The drum family are called membranophones. The name comes from the word "membrane", which means skin. Drums make their sound by vibrating a skin which is stretched tightly over a frame. The frame also acts as the resonator. Drums can be cylindrical (open or closed at the end), double-headed (with skins at both ends), or bowl shaped. There are a very large number of variations to these basic shapes.

The double-sided frame drum (above) is played by rotating the handle. It is sometimes called a prayer drum. Drums like this one are often associated with religious ceremonies and prayers.

The frame drum (right), with its shallow edge and double sides, may have originated in the Middle East. It is also found among the North American Indians and Inuit peoples. The tambourine (see page 11) belongs to this group of drums.

Make a paper prayer drum

This drum is simple to make from stretched paper. It is based on the same principle as the prayer drum shown opposite.

You will need: cardboard tube, approx. 2½ in (6 cm) deep and 4¼ in (11 cm) across • oak tag • pencil • scissors • awl • paintbrush handle • ¾-in (1.5-cm) dowel, 12½ in (32 cm) long • white glue • paints • PVA glue mixed with water • cotton string • two beads • thumbtacks • feathers

1 Draw around cardboard tube twice on oak tag. Cut two circles 1 in (3 cm) larger than tube.

2 Use awl to make ¾-in (1.5-cm) hole in one side of cardboard tube.

Enlarge hole by pushing tapered paintbrush handle into it. Slot dowel through hole and glue to opposite side.

3 Draw and paint design on each paper circle (see page 5). Make scissor cuts all around from edge to inside circle. Paint front and back of paper disks with glue mixture.

4 Stretch sticky paper disks over both sides of cardboard tube frame. Glue around edges. Leave to dry.

5 Cut two lengths of thick cotton string about 2¾ in (7 cm) long. Tie a bead on one end. Attach string to either side of drum with thumbtacks. Decorate with feathers.

Great drums

Drums are often associated with Africa, where they play a very important role. Master drummers provide entertainment and accompaniment for dancing.

The conical *ntenga* drum (shown back right) is from Kenya. It is double-headed, but only the larger head is played. *Ntenga* are usually played in pairs of different sizes. The head and stretchers are made from animal skin. A pattern is made by twisting skin stretchers of different colored fur.

The large waisted drum (below left) comes from Gambia. It is made from hollowed-out wood and animal skin secured by wooden pegs. The smaller, African drum (below center) is a "footed" type, cut from a dried gourd. The double-headed *chigubhu* from Zimbabwe (second from left) is worn around the player's neck so that both ends can be played.

Goblet-shaped pottery drums called *darabuka* come from Islamic North Africa. They are often decorated with painting or inlaid work, like the one from Tunisia shown far right.

Make a skin drum

You will need: large cardboard tube • awl • paintbrush handle • two lengths of ¹/₂-in (1-cm) dowel • dark brown wood stain • black felt-tip pen • brown shoe polish • chamois leather • thick cord • needle and thick thread

Uncured animal skins are usually used for drumheads because they dry hard and taut. They are difficult to find, and most music stores no longer sell them. However, chamois leather can be bought in car accessory shops and works quite well. Cardboard tubes, plastic piping, wooden barrels, or flowerpots make good cylindrical drums. Pottery cooking pots, coconuts, or paint tins are suitable for bowl or vessel drums.

1 Make two holes opposite each other in tube, using awl and paintbrush handle (see page 25). Push ¹/₂-in (1-cm) dowel through both holes so that 1 in (3 cm) sticks out each side. Pierce second pair of holes, at right angles to first. Make these slightly lower down, so that second dowel will push through.

2 Decorate tube by painting with dark brown wood stain and black felt-tip pen. Finish with brown shoe polish.

3 Cut circle of leather 1 in (3 cm) bigger than tube. Soak in water and wring out. Make four evenly spaced holes in edge.

4 Place leather on top of tube. Run cord through one hole and under dowel. Repeat around other dowels. Wrap cord around tube twice. Knot to secure.

5 With needle and thick thread, sew edge of leather to cord rings, stretching gently all around. Leave to dry.

Making music

Making music together is a worldwide human activity and everywhere children are involved. They do not usually have formal lessons, but are introduced to music making from an early age.

In Africa, mothers rock their babies to sleep, singing nonsense songs that imitate drum rhythms. They carry the babies on their back to events where music is played.

Native American children also learn music by copying. They can often reproduce a song perfectly after hearing it only once.

Teenagers are encouraged to go into the wilderness on a "song quest" to find a tune that is uniquely their own.

In Indonesia, children learn the music of the *gamelan* orchestra by attending the puppet theater. From around the age of five, they progress through all the instruments, playing the most difficult ones when they are adult. The most important thing in the *gamelan* orchestra is for every player to contribute to the overall sound.

Make beaters for your drums

All kinds of things can be used as beaters for drums, xylophones, etc. A knitting needle is ready to use, and a dowel can be shaped into a drumstick. Make a head for a bamboo cane from a wooden bead, a metal nut, a cork, or string. Wrap masking tape around the end of a stick if you want to make a soft sound. Use brush bristles to make a rustling noise.

A bow for strings

Traditionally, the best material for a bow is horsehair that has been rubbed with resin. However, horsehair is not easy to find today. A good alternative can be nylon thread, a guitar string, or stretched elastic.

Tie one end of the thread to the end of a thin garden cane. Bend the cane into a gentle arc and tie the loose end of thread to the other end.

When you have made quite a few of the instruments in this book, you may like to gather some friends together to help you make music. You could even form a band or an orchestra to entertain others.

In many cultures, music is based on the natural rhythms of speech. You can use this idea to build up a piece of music that involves as many instruments as you have available.

Begin with some words that you like; for example, "Can you hear the music of the spheres?" Say this sentence over and over again, listening to its rhythm. Start with a steady beat (sticks/large drum/ spike fiddle), then add in instruments like panpipes, guitar, and *gender*. Percussion instruments (shaker/ drum/tambourine) add their own rhythms. Finally, the prayer drum adds its own burst of beats.

Tuning your instruments

If you know where to find the notes of the G major and C major scales on a piano or recorder, it will help you to tune the instruments you make.

G major scale
Piano

C major scale
Recorder

C D E F G A B C

F#

G A B C D E G

MIDDLE

Useful information

Equipment and materials

Most supplies are available in local craft and hobby stores, and even five-and-ten cent stores. The Yellow Pages will have many of the places listed, and you can find the ones closest to you. Here are some that can be contacted.

Leisurecrafts Inc.
3061 Maria Street
Compton, CA 90224
(213) 537-5150

Pearl Paint Co.
1033 E. Oakland Park Boulevard
Ft. Lauderdale, FL 33334
(305) 564-5700

Trost Model & Craft
3129 W. 47th Street
Chicago, IL 60632
(312) 927-1400

The Brighten-Up Shop
618 Central Avenue
Great Falls, MT 59401
(406) 453-8273

S & R Distributing Co.
714 Greenville Boulevard
Greenville, NC 27834
(919) 756-9565

A Hobby Hut
2835 Nostrand Avenue
Brooklyn, NY 11229
(718) 338-2554

Pearl Paint Co.
308 Canal Street
New York, NY 10013
(212) 431-7932

Dupey Management Corp.
P.O. Box 169029
Irving, TX 75063
(214) 929-8595

Thomas Wholesale
5641D General Washington Drive
Alexandria, VA 22312
(703) 820-9790

Craf-T Inc.
P.O. Box 44577
Tacoma, WA 98444
(206) 537-5353

Tri-County Distributors
2785 S. 167th Street
New Berlin, WI 53151
(414) 782-2120

Books

Ardley, Neil.
Music.
New York: Knopf Books for Young Readers, 1989.

Fiarotta, Noel and Phyllis Fiarotta.
Music Crafts for Kids: The How-to Book of Music Discovery.
New York: Sterling, 1993.

Fichter, George S.
American Indian Music and Musical Instruments.
New York: McKay, 1978.

Jackson, Michael.
Making Music: Shake, Rattle & Roll with Instruments You Make Yourself.
New York: HarperCollins, 1993.

Jeunesse, Gallimard.
Musical Instruments: From Flutes Carved of Bone, to Lutes, to Modern Electric Guitars.
New York: Scholastic, 1994.

McLean, Margaret.
Make Your Own Musical Instruments.
Minneapolis, MN: Lerner, 1988.

Morris, Ting and Neil.
Music.
New York: Franklin Watts, 1993.

Oates, Eddie.
Garden Hose Trumpet: And 5 Other Musical Instruments You Can Make.
New York: HarperCollins, 1995.

Wiseman, Ann.
Making Musical Things: Improvised Instruments.
New York: Scribners Young Readers, 1979.

Glossary

aerophone A musical instrument that works by vibrating air against a sharp edge.

amplify To make louder.

bridge A piece of wood or other material over which strings are stretched.

calabash The hard shell of a gourd or other tropical fruit that is used as a container.

ceramic Made of pottery.

chamois leather Soft leather from a sheep, goat, or deer.

chordophone A musical instrument that works by vibrating strings.

conical Cone-shaped.

Coptic Belonging to the Copts, a group of Christians originally from Egypt.

cylindrical In the shape of a cylinder or tube.

flat A musical term that means below the normal pitch of a note.

***gamelan* orchestra** A group of Indonesian musicians who play at religious ceremonies, dances, and puppet plays.

hide Skin of an animal.

ideophone A musical instrument that is designed to use the natural sounds of different materials.

inlaid work A way of decorating a wooden surface by fitting different pieces of colored wood into it.

linguaphone A musical instrument that works by vibrating a "tongue" of metal or other material.

membranophone A musical instrument that works by vibrating a skin, or membrane.

modification A change that makes something work better.

morris dancer Traditional English folk dancer.

Pan The Greek god of woods and pastures.

pitch The quality of a musical note. Pitch is measured by the rate of vibrations.

resonator A box or container that makes a note sound louder.

sharp A musical term that means higher than the normal pitch of a note.

uncured Describes an animal skin before it has been treated to make it supple.

vessel A container such as a pot or jar.

vibrate To move backward and forward very quickly.

Index

Additional photographs:

page 12 (bottom), Christine Osborne Pictures;
page 14 (top), page 22 (right), page 24 (right),
Robert Harding Picture Library.